P

119117

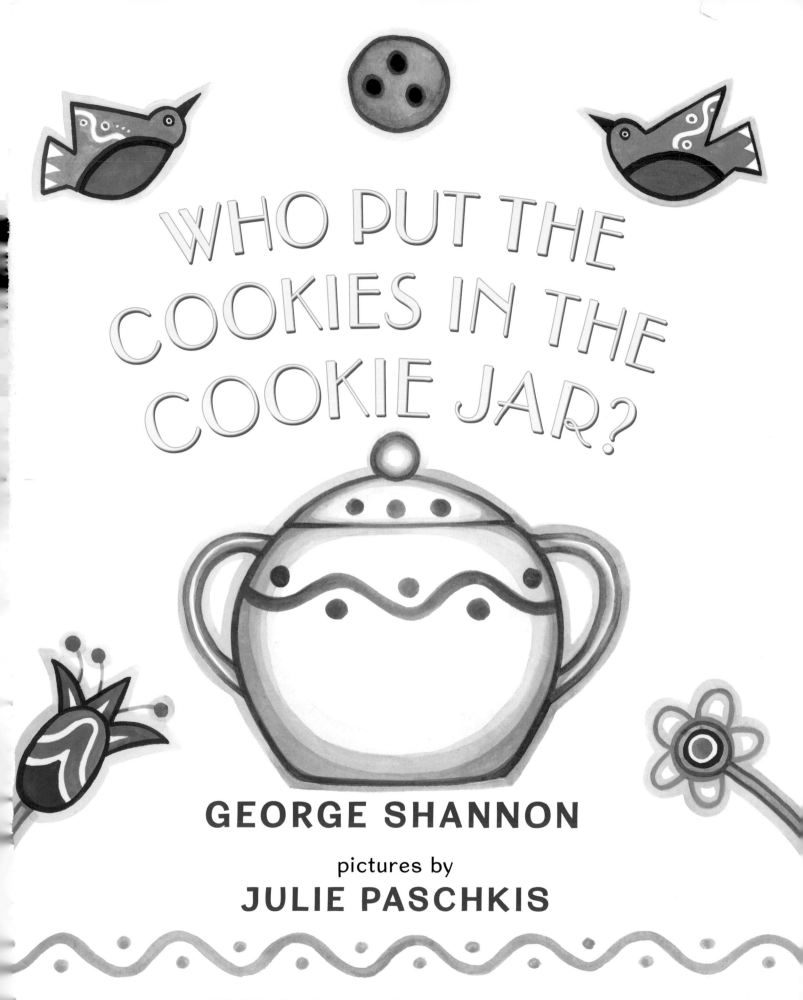

WHO PUT THE COOKIES IN THE COOKIE JAR?

GEORGE SHANNON

pictures by
JULIE PASCHKIS

HENRY HOLT AND COMPANY · NEW YORK

Henry Holt and Company, LLC
Publishers since 1866
175 Fifth Avenue
New York, New York 10010
mackids.com

Library of Congress Cataloging-in-Publication Data
Shannon, George.
Who put the cookies in the cookie jar? / George Shannon ; illustrated by Julie Paschkis. — 1st ed.
p.   cm.
Audience: 3–6.
ISBN 978-0-8050-9197-7 (hardcover)
1. Cookies—Juvenile literature. 2. Baking—Juvenile literature. I. Title.
TX772.S493 2013   641.86'54—dc23   2012010162

First Edition—2013
The artist used Winsor & Newton gouache on Arches paper
to create the illustrations for this book.

Printed in China by Macmillan Production Asia Ltd., Kwun Tong,
Kowloon, Hong Kong (vendor code: PS)

3   5   7   9   10   8   6   4   2

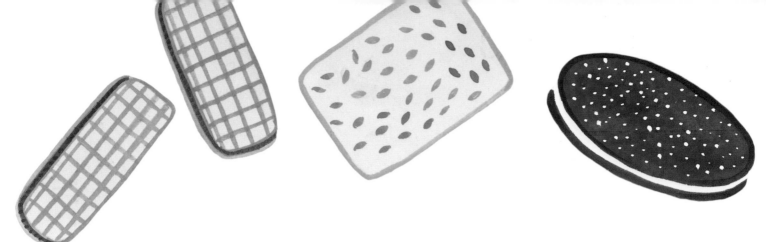

With grateful smiles to Thich Nhat Hanh
—G. S.

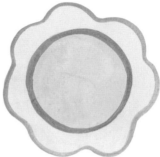

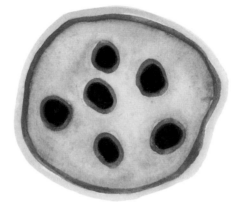

For Benjamin David Kaye
—J. P.

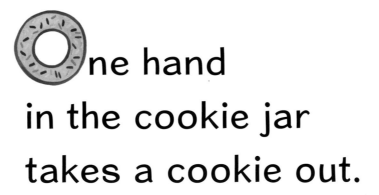One hand
in the cookie jar
takes a cookie out.

How many hands
put the cookie **in**

is what the
world's about.

Hands that mix and stir the dough.

Spoon the clumps into a row.

Hands that make the cookie sheet.

Oven mitts against the heat.

Hands that feed

and milk the cow.

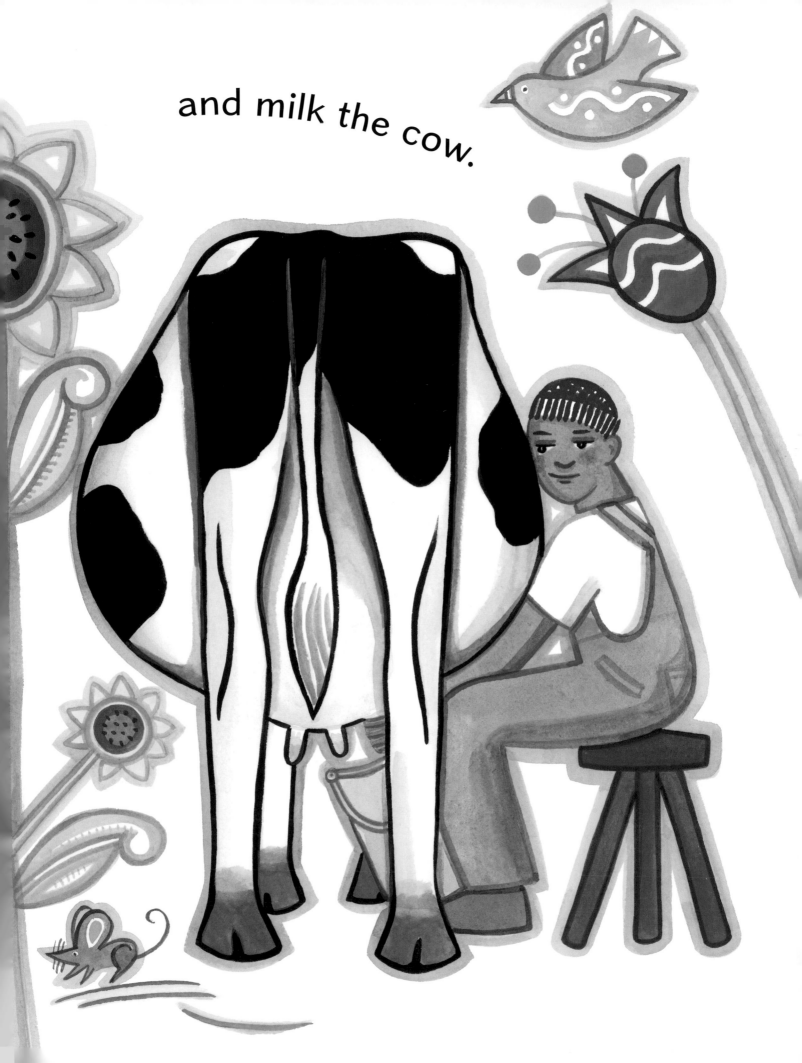

Churn the butter.

Guide the plow.

Hands that sow
and grind the wheat

into flour
for us to eat.

Hands that tend
and feed the hens.

Gather eggs.

Build the pens.

Hands that harvest sugarcane.
Cut and grind.
Load the train.

Hands that load
the trucks

and drive.

Stock the shelves
when things arrive.

Hands that clothe and feed them all.
Heal and teach.
Large and small.

Hands that help
the hands that help
are what the world's about . . .

so **one** can
take it out.

SUGAR COOKIES

1 cup sugar
½ cup unsalted butter, melted
1 egg
2 tablespoons milk
2 teaspoons vanilla
1½ cups all-purpose flour
½ teaspoon baking powder
½ teaspoon salt

- Preheat oven to 375 degrees.
- Grease 2 cookie sheets.
- Combine sugar, melted butter, egg, milk, and vanilla. Beat or stir until smooth.
- In a small bowl, combine flour, baking powder, and salt.
- Add the flour mixture to the sugar mixture and beat or stir until combined.
- Drop teaspoons of dough onto a cookie sheet, and press each cookie down with the bottom of a glass or the palm of your hand.
- Bake 10 to 12 minutes at 375 degrees, until the edges just begin to turn golden brown. Cool for 2 minutes on the cookie sheets, then transfer to cooling racks.

Makes about 3 dozen cookies.

TIP: Sugar cookies are very simple, so they're easy to dress up. Add sprinkles, top with some cinnamon sugar, press a nut into the middle, add chocolate chips—get creative!